S0-ATY-050

Weight Watchers Freestyle Instant Pot

#2019

5-Ingredient Affordable, Quick and Easy WW Smart Points Recipes | Weight Loss, Boost Your Energy and Live a Healthy Life | Lose up 30 Pounds in 21 Days

Megen Soudy

© Copyright 2019 Megen Soudy - All Rights Reserved.

In no way is it legal to reproduce, duplicate, or transmit any part of this document by either electronic means or in printed format. Recording of this publication is strictly prohibited, and any storage of this material is not allowed unless with written permission from the publisher. All rights reserved.

The information provided herein is stated to be truthful and consistent, in that any liability, regarding inattention or otherwise, by any usage or abuse of any policies, processes, or directions contained within is the solitary and complete responsibility of the recipient reader. Under no circumstances will any legal liability or blame be held against the publisher for any reparation, damages, or monetary loss due to the information herein, either directly or indirectly.

Respective authors own all copyrights not held by the publisher.

Legal Notice:

This book is copyright protected. This is only for personal use. You cannot amend, distribute, sell, use, quote or paraphrase any part of the content within this book without the consent of the author or copyright owner. Legal action will be pursued if this is breached.

Disclaimer Notice:

Please note the information contained within this document is for educational and entertainment purposes only. Every attempt has been made to provide accurate, up-to-date and reliable, complete information. No warranties of any kind are expressed or implied. Readers acknowledge that the author is not engaging in the rendering of legal, financial, medical or professional advice.

By reading this document, the reader agrees that under no circumstances are we responsible for any losses, direct or indirect, which are incurred as a result of the use of information contained within this document, including, but not limited to, errors, omissions, or inaccuracies.

Table of contents

Introduction

Recently, US News did a survey that accounted for some of the most prolific diets of recent years and ranked them based on their popularity and effectiveness.

Needless to say, the Weight Watchers Freestyle program came out as one of the most voted and beloved programs out there, with followers claiming that this is one of the most effective methods of effortlessly losing your weight and staying in shape.

Using the meticulously designed Smart Points system, The Weight Watchers Freestyle helps to control your portions and push you towards a healthier and more satisfying diet regime.

The core concept is very simple here if you think about it.

Depending on various factors such as your sex, body weight, age and target weight, a fixed amount of SmartPoints is allocated to you every week.

During that week, you are allowed to eat whatever you want as long as you don't exceed the specified limit.

Every food group and various ingredients are carefully assigned a fixed number of SmartPoints in such a way that will always be inclined to eat healthier food.

And since this book has recipes that can be prepared using the Instant Pot, you will be able to make them in no time and with minimal fuss!

The first chapter of the book focuses on explaining some of the core concepts of the program while the second one will give you an overview of your Instant Pot.

After that, feel free to explore the amazing recipes of this book!

I hope that you will enjoy the contents of the book and be able to fully utilize the potential of the Weight Watchers Freestyle program and bring out the best of you!

Stay safe and God bless!

Chapter 1: Weight Watchers Freestyle Basics

The history of Weight Watchers

The Weight Watchers program was founded by Jean Nidetech in 1963 while living in her home in Queens, New York.

Unlike most of the diets out there though, the origin of Weight Watchers is a very straightforward and down to earth story.

Curious? Well, the program was conceived through a very simple conversation between Nidetech and her friends, who were just simply talking about their cookie addiction!

Through humble beginnings though, the popularity of Weight Watchers has soared and now it is considered as one of the most well-known diets all around!

So, after Jean's meeting at Queens, Jean got very inspired and went on to publish her first book based on this particular topic known as "The Memoir of A Successful Loser The Story of The Weight Watchers." This book was probably the first manuscript that covered the core ideas of Weight Watchers.

Later on, this topic was further explored and expanded up in the book titled "Weight Watchers Program Handbook for Ladies."

In 1989, the Weight Watchers program went through an overhaul and came to be known as the "Exchange-Based diet."

These involved individuals know the amount of food that they could eat from individual food groups, including fats, fruits, dairy, and vegetables.

For example, a "Fat Exchange" could be a tablespoon of olive oil.

If you the plan that you are following allow you to exchange fat, then you could only have 2 tablespoons of oil as salad dressing, which would exhaust your fat exchange for the day.

The primary goal of the exchange program though was to help you control the number of calories consumed.

In 1997 though, the first "Points" system was introduced to the world that was known as the 1-2-3 success program.

This fantastic new system gave members an easy way to track their fat, calories and fiber consumption.

The points system became so popular that it became an integral part of the modern Weight Watchers program that we follow today

The program was even further modified in the early 2000s once the points were changed to Winning Point, this was a very simple modification but it allowed people to incorporate exercise and workout to your points system.

But as time went by, the program evolved even further and the Turn Around program came into the family, that allowed individuals to pick between multiple plans.

The core plan consisted of picking healthy foods from a given sure list, while the Flex plan gave members to eat whatever they wanted to eat as long as they kept track of their pints and stayed within their allocated weekly points limit.

However, in 2009, the Weight Watchers Momentum Plan was introduced, which further refined the points system and helped people understand the process better, and let them know how the points system was helping them prevent overeating.

The program that we follow today is an updated version of the PointsPlus program that was first introduced in 2012, which evolved into the current SmartPoints program that we follow.

Enter "Freestyle"

The Weight Watchers Freestyle Plan is the most evolved version of the program that is designed that came into fruition after 50 years.

The Freestyle plan takes all the good parts of the previous programs and combines them into a very simple program, that uses a "Smart Points" system.

However, before understanding the Freestyle, you should have a good understanding of the core "Weight Watchers" program first.

So, unlike most of the diet, the Weight Watchers won't ask you to follow a strict diet regime that will cancel out all of your desired foods! Instead, it implements a very carefully crafted "Points" system that helps you to maintain and control your food intake in the long run.

Different food groups and ingredients are assigned some Smart Points to help you keep track of your intake.

Throughout the years since the conception of the very first Weight Watchers program, there have been numerous updates to this points system and the one that we are following is called the "SmartPoints" system, which is an overhauled version of the previous "PointsPlus" one.

In 2018 though, the Weight Watchers Organization took another step and updated its Smart Points system with the introduction of the Freestyle program.

The Freestyle program is an extension of the Weight Watchers program, and the core changes are noted down below:

- Rollover Points: This is yet another feature that comes as an exclusive to the Weight Watchers Freestyle program! The "Roll Over" system allows you to transfer a maximum of 4 good daily points from the current week to the next week if you need! So, for example, if you have a current Weekly limit of 120 Smart Points and you used only 116 SmartPoint in the previous week, then you have 4 Roll Over points! Which means in the coming week, you have 124 SmartPoints to consider The Roll Over Points is a grand strategy that helps to prepare you for an upcoming event.

- Weekly Point Allowance: Despite having a change in your daily point allowance, the weekly allowance will remain the same. This means that you will be able to include more food and adjust your plans with greater flexibility.

- About SmartPoints: The updated Freestyle program will still use the same method of calculation. However, your daily SmartPoint allocation will change a bit to balance out the new foods that are all zeroed out now. If you are already a member of the Weight Watchers program, then you may be able to do this with through their designated app, or you may use the apps mentioned in the previous section.

- The new "Zero" Point foods: This is perhaps the most significant change in the new program. Various ingredients and food items that had a significant number of SmartPoints accompanying them have been completely cut down to Zero. This gives you greater freedom when choosing your meal and designing your plans.

What are Smart Points?

As you can already tell, at the heart of this program is the "SmartPoints" system that governs everything. So, it is crucial that you have a good understanding of how Smart Points works.

But before that, let's discuss briefly what "SmartPoints" actually are.

To make things simple and short, Smart Points are essentially a method of counting your daily nutritional intake by associating a set "Value" with the foods that you take based on your nutritional values.

In the Weight Watchers Freestyle program, a certain amount of SmartPoint is associated with certain types of foods and ingredients. This ultimately helps to push your body towards consuming healthier goods.

How Do Smart Points work?

Just to let you know, Smart Points are based on four components of any food:

- Protein
- Sugar
- Saturated Fat
- Calories

That being said, you should know that:

- The more protein your food has, the fewer SmartPoints the value will have
- More sugar and fat will increase the Smart Points value

- The calories of food are considered as the base by which Smart Point values are measured.

While there are several different calculators out there in the web that will help you to measure your daily allocated Smart Points and the Smart Points of the meal that you are having, it's always good to know how to measure them manually.

So, the basic formula goes like this:

Points = (Calories + (Fat x 4) – (Fiber x 10))/50

However, if you want greater accuracy, then you can always refer to the provided list of the common ingredients (and their SP) in the section below.

As for calculating your daily SmartPoints limit, there are several amazing calculators out there that will help you to achieve that. Two good examples are:

http://www.healthyweightforum.org/eng/calculators/ww-points-allowed/

or

http://www.calculator.net/weight-watchers-points-calculator.html

Just to give you an idea though, let's follow an example where we assume that you are a 20-year-old male and have a weight of 70kgs with a height of 5 feet and your target is to lose 10 kg. Your allocated SP will be 30.

However, the best way to calculate your Daily and Weekly Allowance is still through the official Weight Watchers App that is provided when purchasing your membership.

But if you want to experiment with the program for free, then the above-mentioned websites will be able to help you while the following apps will help you as well.

- Ultimate Food Diary App (This app is the only one that has been updated to provide services that resemble the Freestyle meal plan)
- iTrackBites (This is yet another app that is very close to the official WW app. However, this did not support the Freestyle program at the time of writing, but it was supposed to be updated very soon).

This means that you are allowed to eat as much as you want as long as you are not crossing your daily point limit.

The Smart Points Food List

Below is a list of the most common ingredients alongside their associated Smart Point for your convenience.

Food with 0 SP

- Coffee
- Banana
- Apple
- Strawberries
- Chicken Breast
- Salad
- Blueberries
- Grapes
- Tomatoes
- Watermelon
- Egg White
- Lettuce

- Deli Sliced Turkey Breast
- Baby Carrots
- Orange
- Cucumber
- Broccoli
- Water
- Green Beans
- Pineapple
- Corn on The Cob (medium)
- Cherries
- Cantaloupe
- Spinach
- Fresh Fruit
- Raspberries
- Shrimp
- Asparagus
- Celery
- Cherry Tomatoes
- Carrots
- Yogurt
- Peach
- Sweet Red Potatoes
- Pear
- Salsa
- Tuna
- Diet Coke

- Mushrooms
- Onions
- Black Beans
- Blackberries
- Zucchini
- Grape Tomatoes
- Mixed Berries
- Grapefruit
- Nectarine
- Mango
- Mustard

Food with 1 SP

- Sugar
- Almond Milk
- Egg
- Guacamole
- Half and Half
- Salad Dressing

Food with 2 SP

- Cream
- Avocado
- 1 Slice of Bread
- Scrambled Egg with milk/ butter
- Luncheon Meat, deli-sliced or ham (2 ounces)

- 2 t tablespoon of Hummus

Food with 3 SP

- Milk Skimmed
- One tablespoon of Mayonnaise
- Chocolate Chip Cookies
- Sweet potatoes ½ a cup
- 3 ounces of boneless Pork Chop
- 1 ounce of flour Tortilla
- Italian Salad Dressing 2 tablespoon
- Three slices of cooked Turkey Bacon
- 1 cup of Cottage Cheese
- An ounce of crumbled feta

Food with 4 SP

- Olive Oil
- American Cheese 1 slice
- Low Fat Milk 1%, 1 Cup
- Cheddar Cheese 1 ounce
- Red Wine 5 ounce
- ¼ cup of Almond
- 5 ounces of White Wine
- Tortilla Chips 1 ounce
- Shredded Cheddar Cheese
- One tablespoon of honey
- 102 ounces of English Muffin

- Mashed Potatoes

Food with 5 SP

- Butter
- 3 Slices of Cooked Bacon
- Reduced Fat Milk 1 Cup
- Cooked Oatmeal 1 cup
- Plain Baked Potato, 6 ounces
- Regular Beer, 12 ounces
- 1 cup of cooked regular/ whole wheat pasta
- Hamburger Bun
- Ranch Salad Dressing
- Any type of Bagel (2 ounces)
- 1 cup of Spaghetti

Food With 6 SP

- White Rice (6)
- Brown Rice (6)
- Peanut Butter 2 tablespoon (6)
- 1 Whole Cup of Milk (7)
- 20 ounces of French Fries (13)
- 1 cup of cooked Quinoa (6)

New "0" SmartPoint Ingredients

- Peas such as chickpeas, sugar snap peas, black-eyed, etc.

- Beans such as black beans, kidney beans, pinto beans, fat-free refried beans, soybeans, sprouts, etc.
- Lentils
- Corn such as baby corn, sweet corn, corn on the cob
- Skinless Chicken Breast
- Skinless Turkey Breast
- Tofu
- Egg and Egg Whites
- Fish and Shellfish
- Yogurt
- Lean Ground Beef
- Non-Fat and Plain Greek Yogurt
- All Fruits
- All Vegetables

To give you a more detailed look at the list, the following now hold a 0 SmartPoint value.

- Yogurt
- Plain Yogurt
- Greek Yogurt
- Watermelon
- Watercress
- Water Chestnuts
- Stir-Fried Vegetables
- Mixed Vegetables
- Sticks of Vegetables
- Turnips

- Turkey Breast
- Turkey Breast Tenderloin
- Ground Turkey Breast
- Tomato
- Tomato Sauce
- Tofu
- Taro
- Tangerine
- Tangelo
- Starfruit
- Winter and Summer Squash
- Spinach
- Shellfish
- Shallots
- Scallions
- Sauerkraut
- Chicken Satay
- Sashimi
- Salsa
- Salad
- Lentils
- Lime
- Lettuce
- Litchi
- Mangoes
- Mung Dal

- Mushroom Caps
- Nectarine
- Okra
- Onions
- Orange
- Parsley
- Pea Shoot
- Peaches
- Pear
- Pepper
- Pickles
- Pineapple
- Plums
- Pomegranate Seeds
- Pomelo
- Pumpkin
- Pumpkin Puree
- Radish
- Salad Mixed Greens
- Salad Three Bean
- Lemon Zest
- Leek
- Kiwifruit
- Jicama
- Jerk Chicken Breast
- Jackfruit

- Heart of Palm
- Guava
- Mixed Baby Greens
- Ginger Root
- Grape Fruit
- Fruit Cup
- Fruit Cocktail
- Fish Fillet
- Fruit
- Fish
- Figs
- Fennel
- Escarole
- Endive
- Egg Whites
- Eggs
- Apples
- Arrowroot
- Applesauce
- Artichoke
- Artichoke Hearts
- Bamboo Shoots
- Banana
- Beans
- Beets
- Blueberries

- Blackberries

- Broccoli

- Brussels

- Cabbage

- Carrots

- Cauliflower

- Cherries

- Chicken Breast

- Clementine

- Cucumber

- Dragon Fruit

- Egg Substitute

- Dates

And a few more.

Advantages and Disadvantages of Weight Watchers

That being said, some amazing advantages of the Weight Watchers diet include:

- Through the Fitpoints system, you will be able to incorporate exercise into your program and encourage yourself to work out more.

- The SmartPoints itself will encourage you to eat healthy food and prevent overeating.

- The simplicity of the program means that even kids can join the program.

- Through various membership programs, you will be able to get various cooking advice and nutritional tips while sharing your own.

- Unlike many other diets, the Weight Watchers won't impose a strict dietary regime upon you.

On the other hand, some disadvantages that you should know about include:

- The freedom to eat so much might make it difficult for you to control yourself.
- Weekly loss progress might discourage you a bit as it takes a significant amount of time before losing weight.
- Some people might not feel comfortable sharing their personal information in group meetings.
- Keeping track of your SmartPoints throughout the day might get tedious if you don't have the patience.

Chapter 2: Instant Pot Basics

Instant Pot advantages

The Instant Pot comes with a great number of advantages that you should know about!

Below are just some of the core ones.

- **Kill all harmful microorganisms:** Because the Instant Pot can reach extremely high temperatures, it is able to kill most of the bacteria and viruses in food.

- **Less noise and steam:** Traditional pressure cookers have the tendency to fill up the kitchen with lots of steam while creating lots of noise too. Instant Pot's technology, however, is created in such a way that it is able to pressure cook without creating a lot of much steam and not making too much noise either.

- **Helps to preserve nutrients:** Unlike most of the traditional cooking methods out there the Instant Pot requires just the bare minimum amount of water needed to produce sufficient amount of steam to cook the ingredients, this, in turn, allows most of the vitamins and minerals to be preserved while cooking!

- **Saves a lot of time of energy:** Thanks to the pressure-cooking process of the Instant Pot, foods are cooked almost 70% faster than other traditional cooking methods. This process uses much less water while cooking! Since the exterior of the pot is insulated, it dramatically minimizes energy and heat loss, which altogether contributes to the amount of energy saved by minimizing thermal loss.

- **Delayed cooking mechanism:** The delayed cooking mechanism lets the food to stay warm and moist as long as they are in the pot. This lets you serve hot food any time you want!

- Built to last: Since the Instant Pots are essentially made of steel, the appliance is able to withstand for a prolonged time. The construction does not hamper the flavors of the meal too.

And a lot more!

The core functions of your Instant Pot

Contrary to popular belief, using the Instant Pot is actually pretty easy, all you have to do is have a good understanding of the main buttons of the Instant Pot.

In light of that, below is a breakdown of all the ones.

- Sauté: You should go for this button if you want to sauté your vegetables or produces inside your inner pot while keeping the lid open. It is possible to adjust the level of brownness you desire by pressing the modify button as well. As a small tip here, you can very quickly push the Sauté Button followed by the Adjust Button two times to simmer your food.

- Keep Warm/Cancel: Using this button, you will be able to turn your pressure cooker off. Alternatively, you can use the adjust button to keep maintaining a warm temperature ranging from 293 degrees F (on average) to 332-degree F (at more) degree Celsius depending on what you need.

- Manual: This is pretty much an all-rounder button which gives a higher level of flexibility to the user. Using this button followed by the + or – buttons, you will be able to set the exact duration of cooking time which you require.

- Soup: This mode will set the cooker to a high-pressure mode giving 30 minutes of cooking time (at normal); 40 minutes (at more); 20 minutes (at less)

- Meat/Stew: This mode will set the cooker to a high-pressure mode giving 35 minutes of cooking time (at normal); 45 minutes (at more); 20 minutes (at less)

- Bean/Chili: This mode will set the cooker to a high-pressure mode giving 30 minutes of cooking time (at normal); 40 minutes (at more); 25 minutes (at less)

- Poultry: This mode will set the cooker to a high-pressure mode giving 15 minutes of cooking time (at normal); 30 minutes (at more); 5 minutes (at less)

- Rice: This is a fully automated mode which cooks rice on low pressure. It will adjust the timer all by itself depending on the amount of water/rice present in the inner cooking pot.

- Multi-Grain: This mode will set the cooker to a high-pressure mode giving 40 minutes of cooking time (at normal); 45 minutes (at more); 20 minutes (at less)

- Porridge: This mode will set the cooker to a high-pressure mode giving 20 minutes of cooking time (at normal); 30 minutes (at more); 15 minutes (at less)

- Steam: This will set your pressure cooker to high pressure with 10 minutes of cooking time at normal. 15 minutes cook time at more and 3 minutes cook time at less. Keep in mind that it is advised to use this model with a steamer basket or rack for best results.

- Slow Cooker: This button will normally set the cooker at 4-hour mode. However, you change the temperature by keeping it at 190-201-degree Fahrenheit (at low); 194-205-degree Fahrenheit (at normal); 199-210-degree Fahrenheit (at high);

- Pressure: This button allows you to alter between high and low-pressure settings.

- Yogurt: This setting should be used when you are in the mood for making yogurt in individual pots or jars

- Timer: This button will allow you to either decrease or increase the time by using the timer button and pressing the + or – buttons.

Learning to clean your Instant Pot

As you keep on using your Instant Pot, you are bound to accumulate some dirt and debris all around. In order to ensure that your appliance stays in tip-top shape, it is essential that you keep your appliance as clean and tidy as possible.

Despite popular belief, cleaning your Instant Pot is actually pretty easy. The core idea is to tackle each component differently.

So, let me break it down for you.

- Condensation Collector: The condensation collector is needed to be cleaned frequently. The process very straightforward, just remove and wash it under cold water.

- Anti-Block Shield and Sealing Ring: The Anti-Block Shield and Sealing Ring are both made of very high-quality heat-resistant materials and can be washed with warm, soapy water. Make sure to dry them before putting them back into place.

- The Lid: The lid of the Instant Pot is dishwasher safe, so you can just remove it and wash it in your dishwasher. However, make sure to remove the sealing ring and anti-block shield before cleaning the lid.

- Stainless Steel Inner Pot and Rack: The inner pot of your Instant Pot is made of stainless steel, food-grade 304 and no chemical coating. Which basically means that it is extremely durable and is designed to last for years to come! It is easy to clean it too, just use non-abrasive stainless-steel cleaner and wipe it gently. Alternatively, you may soak it in white vinegar for 5 minutes and rinse it well.

- The Base and Heating element: The base of the cooker is where the heating element and all other circuits are situated, so it is strictly prohibited to put the base in the dishwasher. However, you may still clean it by taking a damp cloth and wiping it gently. The inside can be cleaned by a slightly wet cloth.

Chapter 3: Hearty Tips for the journey

Now that all the basics are covered, let me share some tips with you that will help you to make your Weight Watchers journey even more enjoyable and fruitful.

- Make sure that you have good control over your portions. Having a good understanding of common units such as ounces, cups are essential to making meal plans.

- While you are on Weight Watchers, make sure to skip over "Diet" drinks and beverages as they are packed with artificial sweeteners, which are unhealthy for your body.

- Keep in mind that while practicing meal control, you should never skip on your daily exercise! Even if it's for just 5-10 minutes, try to do exercise daily.

- When you are eating outside, try to split your meals with an acquaintance. This will lower your calorie intake while maintaining a friendly environment.

- With experience, try to explore new recipes and ingredients as they will help you enjoy the program even more!

Chapter 4: Breakfast

Baby Carrots

Serving: 4

Prep Time: 5 minutes

Cook Time: 5 minutes

Ingredients

- 1 pound of baby carrots
- 1 cup of water
- 1 tablespoon of clarified ghee
- 1 tablespoon of chopped up fresh mint leaves
- Sea flavored vinegar as needed

How To

1. Place a steamer rack on top of your pot and add the carrots
2. Add water
3. Lock up the lid and cook at HIGH pressure for 2 minutes
4. Do a quick release
5. Pass the carrots through a strainer and drain them
6. Wipe the insert clean
7. Return the insert to the pot and set the pot to Sauté mode
8. Add clarified butter and allow it to melt
9. Add mint and Sauté for 30 seconds
10. Add carrots to the insert and Sauté well
11. Remove them and sprinkle with a bit of flavored vinegar on top
12. Enjoy!

Nutrition Values (Per Serving)

- Calories: 131
- Fat: 10g
- Carbohydrates: 11g
- Protein: 1g

Hearty Squashed Salad

Serving: 4

Prep Time: 10 minutes

Cook Time: 15 minutes

Ingredients

- 1 apple, cored, peeled, cut into wedges
- 1 cup of vegetable stock, low sodium
- 1 acorn squash, halved and cut into wedges
- 2 tablespoon of coconut sugar
- 2 teaspoons of avocado oil

How To

1. Add apple, stock, sugar, squash, and oil to the pot
2. Toss well and lock up the lid
3. Cook on HIGH pressure for 15 minutes
4. Perform a quick release
5. Divide amongst serving plates and enjoy!

Nutrition Values (Per Serving)

- Calories: 180
- Fat: 5g
- Carbohydrates: 15g
- Protein: 8g

Butternut and Ginger Mash

Serving: 8

Prep Time: 10 minutes

Cook Time: 15 minutes

Ingredients

- 2 pounds of butternut squash, peeled and chopped
- 2 whole eggs
- 2 cups of water
- 1 cup of coconut milk
- 2 tablespoon of coconut sugar
- 1 teaspoon of cinnamon powder
- ½ a teaspoon of ginger powder

How To

1. Add 1 cup of water to your Instant Pot
2. Add steamer basket and add squash pieces
3. Lock up the lid and cook on HIGH pressure for 5 minutes
4. Perform a quick release and remove the lid
5. Drain the squash cubes and transfer them to a bowl
6. Add sugar, milk, cinnamon, eggs, and ginger and mash the whole mixture, whisk well
7. Pour the mixture into ramekins
8. Add remaining water to your Instant Pot
9. Place steamer basket and add the ramekins
10. Lock up the lid and cook on HIGH pressure for 14 minutes
11. Release the pressure naturally over 10 minutes
12. Serve and enjoy!

Nutrition Values (Per Serving)

- Calories: 182
- Fat: 1g
- Carbohydrates: 18g
- Protein: 3g

All-Round Frittata

Serving: 6

Prep Time: 10 minutes

Cook Time: 5 minutes

Ingredients

- 2 tablespoons of almond milk
- Just a pinch of pepper
- 6 eggs, cracked and whisked
- 2 tablespoons of parsley, chopped
- 1 tablespoon of low-fat cheese, shredded
- 1 cup of water
- 1 teaspoon parsley

How To

1. Take a bowl and add eggs, almond milk, pepper, cheese, and parsley. Whisk well
2. Take a plan that would fit in your Instant Pot and grease with cooking spray
3. Pour the egg mixture into the pan
4. Add a cup of water to your pot and place a steamer basket
5. Add the pan in the basket
6. Lock up the lid and cook on HIGH pressure for 5 minutes
7. Release the pressure naturally over 10 minutes
8. Remove the lid and divide the frittata amongst serving plates
9. Enjoy!

Nutrition Values (Per Serving)

- Calories: 200
- Fat: 4g
- Carbohydrates: 17g
- Protein: 6g

Awesome Baked Eggs

Serving: 4

Prep Time: 10 minutes

Cook Time: 25 minutes

Ingredients

- Olive oil
- 4 whole eggs
- 4 ham slices
- 8 tablespoon of cream cheese
- Dash of French herb mix
- Salt and pepper to needed

How To

1. Place a steamer basket in your Instant Pot
2. Add a cup of water
3. Brush 4 ramekins and grease with olive oil, keep it on the side
4. Add a sliced ham, 2 tablespoons of cream cheese, a dash of the mixed herb into each of the ramekins
5. Crack eggs into each of the ramekins as well
6. Season with pepper and salt
7. Place on the steam rack
8. Lock up the lid and cook on LOW pressure for 25 minutes
9. Release pressure naturally over 10 minutes
10. Serve and enjoy!

Nutrition (Per Serving)

- Calories: 246
- Fat: 19g
- Carbohydrates: 4g
- Protein: 15g

Simple Breakfast Cobbler

Serving: 4

Prep Time: 10 minutes

Cooking Time: 10 minutes

Ingredients:

- 1 apple, chopped and cored
- 1 pear, chopped
- 1 plum, chopped
- 2 tablespoons pecans, chopped
- 2 tablespoons sunflower seeds
- ¼ cup coconut, shredded
- 3 tablespoons coconut oil
- ½ teaspoon ground cinnamon
- 2 tablespoons honey

Directions:

1. Set your pot to Sauté mode and add oil, let it heat up
2. Add honey, plum, pear and apple
3. Stir and lock lid
4. Cook on STEAM mode for 10 minutes
5. Quick release pressure
6. Divide fruit mix between serving plates and sprinkle coconut, pecans and sunflower seeds
7. Serve and enjoy!

Nutritional Contents:

- Calories: 154
- Fat: 2g
- Carbohydrates: 5g
- Protein: 3g

Poblano Cheese Egg Frittata

Serving: 2

Prep Time: 10 minutes

Cook Time: 25 minutes

Ingredients

- 4 whole eggs
- 1 cup of half and half cream
- 10 ounces green chilies, diced
- ½-1 teaspoon of salt
- ½ a teaspoon of ground cumin
- 1 cup of Mexican blend shredded cheese
- ¼ cup of chopped cilantro

How To

1. Take a bowl and beat eggs and a half and half
2. Add diced green chilis, salt, cumin and ½ cup of shredded cheese
3. Pour the mixture into 6 inches greased metal pan and cover with foil
4. Add 2 cups of water to the Instant Pot
5. Place trivet in the pot and place the pan in the trivet
6. Lock up the lid and cook on HIGH pressure for 20 minutes
7. Release the pressure naturally over 10 minutes
8. Scatter half cup of the cheese on top of your quiche and broil for a while until the cheese has melted
9. Enjoy!

Nutrition Values (Per Serving)

- Calories: 257
- Fat: 19g
- Carbohydrates: 6g
- Protein: 14g

Omelette Quiche

Serving: 6

Prep Time: 5 minutes

Cook Time: 10 minutes

Ingredients

- 6 large eggs, beaten
- ½ cup milk
- 1/8 teaspoon Himalayan salt
- 1/8 teaspoon black pepper, ground
- 8 ounces bacon, chopped
- ¾ cups red and green pepper, diced
- 3 spring onions, chopped
- ¾ cup cheddar cheese, grated

How To

1. Add the listed ingredients to your Instant Pot (Except cheese)
2. Stir well
3. Sprinkle cheese on top
4. Lock up the lid and cook on HIGH pressure for 10 minutes
5. Perform quick release
6. Enjoy!

Nutrition (Per Serving)

- Calories: 333
- Fat: 22g
- Carbohydrates: 17g
- Protein: 17g

Paprika Eggs Delight

Serving: 6

Prep Time: 10 minutes

Cooking Time: 5 minutes

Ingredients:

- ½ teaspoon paprika
- 6 whole eggs
- ¼ teaspoon salt
- Pinch of pepper
- 1 and ½ cups of water

Directions:

1. Add water to Instant Pot
2. Crack an egg into the baking dish
3. Cover dish with foil and place on a rack, place the rack in Instant Pot
4. Lock lid and cook on HIGH pressure for 4 minutes
5. Quick-release pressure
6. Remove the loaf of eggs and finely diced
7. Stir in spices and serve
8. Enjoy!

Nutritional Contents:

- Calories: 62
- Fat: 4g
- Carbohydrates: 0g
- Protein: 5g

Sweet Bacon Ranch Potatoes

Serving: 6

Prep Time: 3 minutes

Cooking Time: 12 minutes

Ingredients:

- 3 bacon strips, cut
- 2 teaspoons parsley, dried
- 2 pounds sweet potatoes, scrubbed and cubed
- 1/3 cup ranch dressing
- 2 tablespoons water
- 1 teaspoon salt and garlic powder

Directions:

1. Add bacon, potatoes, parsley, garlic powder, water and salt to your instant pot
2. Lock lid properly and cook on High pressure for 7 minutes
3. Release the pressure naturally for 10 minutes
4. Add ranch dressing on top
5. Serve and enjoy!

Nutritional Contents:

- Calories: 227
- Fat: 12g
- Carbohydrates: 5g
- Protein: 24g

Hot Chocolate Oatmeal

Serving:

Prep Time: 10 minutes

Cooking Time: 1 to 2 hours

Ingredients:

- 1 cup steel cut oats
- ½ cup coconut milk
- 1 teaspoon vanilla
- 1 teaspoon coconut palm sugar
- 1 teaspoon cocoa powder
- 4 cups water
- 8 drops liquid stevia

Directions:

1. Take a large bowl and mix vanilla, milk, water and stevia all together
2. Whisk in the cocoa, sugar and salt
3. Stir in the oats
4. Oil the inside of the slow cooker so it does not stick and pour the mixture in
5. Select Low for 1 to 2 hours
6. Keep warm before leaving it
7. Add shaved dark chocolate on top
8. Serve and enjoy!

Nutritional Contents:

- Calories: 126
- Fat: 8g
- Carbohydrates: 12.4g
- Protein: 2.7g

Egg and Spinach Bowl

Serving:

Prep Time: 5 minutes

Cooking Time: 20 minutes

Ingredients:

- 8 egg whites
- 1 cup baby spinach, chopped or torn
- 1 whole egg
- ½ cup tomatoes, diced
- ½ teaspoon black pepper
- ¼ cup feta cheese
- Sea salt

Directions:

1. Preheat your oven to 350 degree
2. Whisk all ingredients together
3. Lightly mist 4 ramekins with non-stick cooking spray
4. Take a cookie sheet and place your ramekin on top of that
5. Bake for 20 minutes
6. Serve hot and enjoy!

Nutritional Contents:

- Calories: 84
- Fat: 2g
- Carbohydrates: 6g
- Protein: 11g

Kale and Carrots Mix

Serving: 5

Prep Time: 10 minutes

Cook Time: 30 minutes

Ingredients

- 10 ounces kale, chopped
- 1 tablespoon ghee
- 1 medium onion, sliced
- 3 medium carrots, cut in half-inch pieces
- 5 garlic cloves, peeled and chopped
- ½ cup chicken broth
- Fresh pepper
- Vinegar as needed
- ½ teaspoon red pepper flakes

How To

1. Set your pot to Sauté mode and add ghee, allow the ghee to melt
2. Add chopped onion and carrots and sauté for a while
3. Add garlic and Sauté for a while
4. Pile the kale on top
5. Pour chicken broth and season with pepper
6. Lock up the lid and cook on HIGH pressure for 8 minutes
7. Release the pressure naturally over 10 minutes
8. Open and give it a nice stir
9. Add vinegar and sprinkle the pepper flakes
10. Enjoy!

Nutrition Values (Per Serving)

- Calories: 41
- Fat: 2g
- Carbohydrates: 5g
- Protein: 2g

Chapter 5: Beef and Pork

Hearty Beef Dish

Servings: 6

Prep Time: 10 minutes

Cook Time: 75 minutes

Ingredients

- 1 tablespoons oil
- 2 pounds beef chuck roast, cut into cubes
- Salt and pepper to taste
- 2 tablespoons cumin powder
- 1 tablespoon paprika
- 1 cup beef broth
- 8 ounces Portobello mushrooms, chopped
- 1 tablespoon onion powder
- 1 can (14.5 ounces) tomato paste
- 1 can (14.5 ounces) tomatoes, crushed

How To

1. Set your pot to sauté mode and add oil, let the oil heat up
2. Add beef chuck roast and sauté until lightly golden on all sides
3. Season with salt and pepper
4. Stir in remaining ingredients and lock lid
5. Cook on MEAT/STEW mode for 60 minutes
6. Release pressure naturally over 10 minutes
7. Serve and enjoy!

Nutritional Values (Per Serving)

- Calories: 373
- Fat: 15g
- Carbohydrates: 15g
- Protein: 44g

Beef and Tomato Platter

Servings: 6

Prep Time: 10 minutes

Cook Time: 25 minutes

Ingredients

- 2 pounds beef fillet, chopped
- 3 onions, finely chopped
- 3 jalapeno peppers, chopped
- 1 chili pepper, chopped
- 1 cup cherry tomatoes, sliced
- 4 tablespoons butter, melted
- 2 tablespoons oil
- 4 cups beef broth

Spices

- 1 teaspoon salt
- ½ fresh ground black pepper
- 1 teaspoon dried parsley
- 1 teaspoon chili powder

How To

1. Rinse the meat under cold running water and pat it dries with kitchen paper
2. Cut into bite-sized pieces and keep it on the side
3. Set your Instant Pot to Sauté mode and grease the inner pot with oil
4. Make a layer of chopped meat, add onions, chopped peppers, tomatoes on top of one another
5. Drizzle melted butter on top and sprinkle salt, pepper, chili powder, and parsley
6. Pour broth and lock lid
7. Cook on HIGH pressure for 25 minutes
8. Quick-release pressure
9. Serve and enjoy!

Nutritional Values (Per Serving)

- Calories: 379
- Fat: 17g
- Carbohydrates: 52g
- Protein: 10g

Sirloin Steak

Serving: 3

Prep Time: 10 minutes

Cook Time: 10 minutes

Ingredients

- 8 ounce of beef sirloin steak, trimmed and fat removed, cut into medium-sized cubes
- ½ a cup of red onion, chopped
- ¼ cup of tomatoes, chopped
- ¾ cup of fat-free cheddar, grated
- 2 tablespoon of coconut cream
- 7 tablespoons of salsa
- 1 tablespoon of olive oil
- 2 tablespoons of cilantro, chopped
- 2 cups beef broth

How To

1. Set your pot to Sauté mode
2. Add oil and allow the oil to heat up
3. Add steak cubes and stir fry them for 3 minutes until brown
4. Add onions, tomatoes, cream, broth and toss well
5. Lock up the lid and cook on HIGH pressure for 7 minutes
6. Release the pressure naturally over 10 minutes
7. Divide into bowls and sprinkle cheese, salsa, cilantro on top
8. Serve and enjoy!

Nutrition Values (Per Serving)

- Calories: 251
- Fat: 4g
- Carbohydrates: 16g
- Protein: 7g

Balsamic Flavored Beef

Serving: 8

Prep Time: 5 minutes

Cook Time: 55 minutes

Ingredients

- 3-pound chuck roast
- 3 cloves garlic, thinly sliced
- 1 tablespoon oil
- 1 teaspoon flavored vinegar
- ½ teaspoon pepper
- ½ teaspoon rosemary
- 1 tablespoon butter
- ½ teaspoon thyme
- ¼ cup balsamic vinegar
- 1 cup beef broth

How To

1. Cut slits in the roast and stuff garlic slices all over
2. Take a bowl and add flavored vinegar, rosemary, pepper, thyme and rub the mixture over the roast
3. Set your pot to Sauté mode and add oil, allow the oil to heat up
4. Add roast and brown both sides (5 minutes each side)
5. Take the roast out and keep it on the side
6. Add butter, broth, balsamic vinegar and deglaze the pot
7. Transfer the roast back and lock up the lid, cook on HIGH pressure for 40 minutes
8. Perform a quick release
9. Remove the lid and serve!

Nutrition (Per Serving)

- Calories: 393
- Fat: 15g
- Carbohydrates: 25g
- Protein: 37g

Spicy Braised Beef

Serving: 9

Prep Time: 5 minutes

Cooking Time: 60 minutes

Ingredients:

- 5 cloves garlic
- ½ medium onion
- 1 lime, juiced
- 2 tablespoons chipotle, in adobo sauce
- 1 tablespoon ground cumin
- 1 tablespoon ground oregano
- ½ teaspoon ground cloves
- 1 cup of water
- 3 pounds beef eye of round, all fat trimmed and chopped into 3-inch pieces
- 2 and ½ teaspoons salt
- Pepper to taste
- 1 teaspoon oil
- 3 bay leaves

Directions:

1. Add cloves, water, chipotle, oregano, cumin, lime juice, onion, garlic to a blender and blend until smooth
2. Season meat with salt and pepper
3. Set your pot to Sauté mode and heat up the oil and add meat to the pot, brown both sides
4. Pour blended sauce and mix in bay leaves
5. Lock lid and cook on HIGH pressure for 1 hour
6. Naturally, release the pressure over 10 minutes
7. Remove meat and shred it
8. Mix the shredded meat with ½ cup of the cooking liquid from the Instant Pot
9. Enjoy!

Nutritional Contents:

- Calories: 153
- Fat: 5g
- Carbohydrates: 10g
- Protein: 24g

Pork Green Chili

Servings: 8

Prep Time: 5 minutes

Cook Time: 90 minutes

Ingredients

- 3 pounds of pork shoulder
- 1 and ½ teaspoons cumin
- Salt and pepper as needed
- 3 tablespoons bacon fat
- 1 onion, chopped
- 1 can crushed tomatoes
- 2 milk hatch green chilies
- 2 hot hatch green chilies
- 1 avocado, sliced
- Sour cream, garnish
- 1 and ½ cups of chicken broth

How To

1. Season pork with cumin, salt, and pepper. Keep it on the side
2. Set your pot to Sauté mode and add bacon fat, melt it
3. Sauté onions and add the seasoned pork
4. Stir cook for 3 minutes
5. Add chicken broth, tomatoes and chilies
6. Lock lid and cook on HIGH pressure for 90 minutes
7. Quick-release pressure
8. Shred the pork meat using forks
9. Serve and enjoy with garnish avocado slices and sour cream
10. Enjoy!

Nutritional Values (Per Serving)

- Calories: 586
- Fat: 40g
- Carbohydrates: 6g
- Protein: 48g

Paprika Pork Chops

Serving: 4

Prep Time: 10 minutes

Cook Time: 10 minutes

Ingredients

- 4 pork chops, boneless
- 1 tablespoon of olive oil
- 1 cup of chicken stock, low sodium
- Pinch of black pepper
- 1 teaspoon of sweet paprika

How To

1. Set your pot to Sauté mode and add oil
2. Allow the oil to heat up, add pork chops and brown for a few minutes
3. Add paprika, pepper, and stock to your pot
4. Lock up the lid and cook on HIGH pressure for 5 minutes
5. Release the pressure naturally over 10 minutes
6. Open the lid and divide amongst serving plates
7. Enjoy!

Nutrition Values (Per Serving)

- Calories: 362
- Fat: 4g
- Carbohydrates: 19g
- Protein: 11g

Low Carb Lime and Ginger Pork

Serving: 10

Prep Time: 10 minutes

Cooking Time: 4-7 hours

Ingredients:

- 1 tablespoon avocado oil
- 2 and ½ pounds pork loin
- Salt and pepper to taste
- 2 tablespoons low carb brown sugar
- 1 teaspoon stevia drops
- ¼ cup tamari
- 1 tablespoon Worcestershire sauce
- Juice of 1 lime
- 2 garlic cloves, minced
- 1 tablespoon fresh ginger
- Fresh cilantro

Directions:

1. Set your pot to Sauté mode and add oil, let the oil heat up
2. Season pork with salt and pepper and add brown sugar to the pot
3. Take a bowl and whisk in remaining ingredients except for cilantro and pour it over pork
4. Lock lid and cook on slow cook mode
5. Cook for 4-7 hours on HIGH pressure
6. Naturally, release the pressure over 10 minutes
7. Garnish with cilantro
8. Serve and enjoy!

Nutritional Contents:

- Calories: 292
- Fat: 16g
- Carbohydrates: 5g
- Protein: 31g

Pork and Cauliflower Gravy

Serving: 6

Prep Time: 10 minutes

Cooking Time: 65 minutes

Ingredients:

- 1 onion, chopped
- 4 cloves garlic, crushed and minced
- 4 cups cauliflower, chopped
- 2 ribs of celery
- Salt and pepper to taste
- 3-pound pork roast
- 8 ounces oyster mushrooms, sliced
- 2 tablespoons coconut oil
- 2 tablespoons ghee

Directions:

1. Add onion, garlic, cauliflower, celery to Instant Pot
2. Put pork roast on top
3. Season with salt and pepper
4. Add 2 cups of water
5. Lock lid and cook on HIGH pressure 60 minutes
6. Quick-release pressure
7. Transfer roast to baking pan
8. Add pan to oven and bake for 5 minutes at 400 degrees F
9. Prepare gravy by transferring the remaining contents from the pot to a blender
10. Blend until smooth
11. Set your pot to Sauté mode and add coconut oil and ghee
12. Add mushrooms and blended mixture
13. Cook for 5 minutes
14. Serve pot roast with mushroom gravy and enjoy!

Nutritional Contents:

- Calories: 697
- Fat: 56g
- Carbohydrates: 8g
- Protein: 81g

Ham and Cabbage Bowl

Serving: 6

Prep Time: 15 minutes

Cook Time: 15 minutes

Ingredients

- 1 cabbage, chopped
- 1 onion, chopped
- 1 red bell pepper, chopped
- 2 small carrots, chopped
- 2 cups lean ham, diced
- 2 bay leaves
- 1 teaspoon all-purpose flour
- 1 teaspoon garlic, granulated
- 1 tablespoon dried parsley
- 1 teaspoon seasoned flavored vinegar
- 6 cups chicken stock
- Parmesan cheese for serving

How To

1. Chop up the cabbage, red bell pepper, onion, ham, and carrots
2. Add the onion, cabbage, and red bell pepper to the Instant Pot
3. Add chopped ham, carrots alongside bay leaves
4. Sprinkle seasoning flavored vinegar on top, all-purpose flour, dried parsley, and granulated garlic
5. Lock up the lid and cook on HIGH pressure for 15 minutes
6. Release the pressure naturally over 10 minutes
7. Serve hot with grated parmesan on top
8. Enjoy!

Nutrition Values (Per Serving)

- Calories: 296
- Fat: 25g
- Carbohydrates: 2g
- Protein: 17g

Acorn Pork Chops

Serving: 4

Prep Time: 10 minutes

Cook Time: 10 minutes

Ingredients

- 2 tablespoons of clarified butter
- 4 pieces of ½ inch thick bone-in pork loin or rib
- ½ teaspoon of salt
- ½ teaspoon pepper
- 2 medium-sized acorn squash, peeled and deseeded, gently cut into eighths
- 3 tablespoons of dried sage
- ½ a teaspoon of dried thyme
- ½ teaspoon of ground cinnamon
- ¾ cup of chicken broth

How To

1. The first step here is to set your pot to Sauté mode and melt in 1 tablespoon of butter
2. Season your chops with pepper and salt and toss them in your pot and cook for 4 minutes
3. Transfer the chops to a plate
4. Then, add the chops to the Instant Pot in a single layer and toss in the squash, sprinkle some thyme, sage, and cinnamon all over
5. Pour in the broth
6. Lock up the lid and let it cook for about 10 minutes at high pressure
7. Quick-release the pressure and transfer the chops to a plate
8. Mound the squash around them nicely and ladle up the sauce (if any) all over the chops

Nutrition Values (Per Serving)

- Calories: 348
- Fat: 18g
- Carbohydrates: 2g
- Protein: 42g

Jamaican Pork Roast

Serving: 4

Prep Time: 5 minutes

Cooking Time: 45 minutes

Ingredients:

- 1 cup beef broth
- 1 tablespoon olive oil
- ¼ cup Jamaican jerk spice blend
- 4 ounces of pork shoulder

Directions:

1. Rub roast with olive oil and spice blend
2. Set your pot to Sauté mode and add meat, brown all sides
3. Pour beef broth
4. Lock lid and cook on HIGH pressure for 45 minutes
5. Quick-release pressure
6. Shred pork and serve!

Nutritional Contents:

- Calories: 308
- Fat: 18g
- Carbohydrates: 5g
- Protein: 31g

Heartfelt Root Chili

Serving: 4

Prep Time: 10 minutes

Cook Time: 10 minutes

Ingredients

- 10 ounces of beets, sliced
- 1 cup of cooked ground beef
- 1 and a 1/3 cup carrot, diced
- 1 and a 1/3 cups sweet potatoes, peeled and sliced
- 10 and a 2/3 ounce of pumpkin
- 1 teaspoon of dried rosemary
- 1 teaspoon of sea salt
- 2 teaspoons of dried basil
- 2/3 teaspoon of cinnamon
- 2 cups of beef bone broth
- 1 and a 1/3 tablespoon of Apple Cider Vinegar

How To

1. Add beets to a food processor and puree
2. Transfer the beets to your Instant Pot
3. Add the rest of the ingredients
4. Lock up the lid and cook on HIGH pressure for 10 minutes
5. Release the pressure naturally over 10 minutes
6. Enjoy!

Nutrition Values (Per Serving)

- Calories: 271
- Fat: 20g
- Carbohydrates: 5g
- Protein: 13g

Chapter 6: Poultry

Lime and Chicken Chili

Servings: 8

Prep Time: 5 minutes

Cook Time: 15 minutes

Ingredients

- 2 pounds chicken breasts, bones removed
- ½ cup lime juice
- 1 and ½ teaspoons chili powder
- 1 teaspoon cumin
- 1 teaspoon onion powder
- 6 cloves garlic, minced
- ½ teaspoon liquid smoke
- Salt and pepper to taste

How To

1. Add the listed ingredients to your Instant Pot and stir
2. Lock lid and cook on HIGH pressure for 15 minutes
3. Quick-release the pressure
4. Shred the chicken meat and serve
5. Enjoy!

Nutritional Values (Per Serving)

- Calories: 207
- Fat: 10g
- Carbohydrates: 3g
- Protein: 24g

White Chicken Chili

Servings: 6

Prep Time: 5 minutes

Cook Time: 20 minutes

Ingredients

- 2 tablespoons oil
- 2 pounds chicken thighs
- 1 onion, diced
- 3 cloves garlic, minced
- 1 cup chicken broth
- 2 cans (14.5 ounces each) northern beans, undrained
- 1 cup corn kernels
- 1 can (14.5 ounces) green chilies, chopped
- 1 can (14.5 ounces) condensed cream of chicken soup
- 1 cup Monterey Jack cheese, grated
- Salt and pepper to taste

How To

1. Set your Instant Pot to Sauté mode and add oil.
2. Stir in chicken thighs, garlic, and onions
3. Sauté until fragrant
4. Add remaining ingredients and stir
5. Lock lid and cook on HIGH pressure for 15 minutes
6. Release pressure naturally over 10 minutes
7. Serve and enjoy!

Nutritional Values (Per Serving)

- Calories: 608
- Fat: 32g
- Carbohydrates: 38g
- Protein: 41g

Carrot and Cucumbers with Duck

Serving: 8

Prep Time: 10 minutes

Cook Time: 40 minutes

Ingredients

- 1 duck, cut up into medium pieces
- 1 chopped cucumber, chopped
- 1 tablespoon of low sodium vegetable stock
- 2 carrots, chopped
- 2 cups of water
- Black pepper as needed
- The 1-inch ginger piece, grated

How To

1. Add duck pieces to your Instant Pot
2. Add cucumber, stock, carrots, water, ginger, pepper and stir
3. Lock up the lid and cook on LOW pressure for 40 minutes
4. Release the pressure naturally
5. Serve and enjoy!

Nutrition Values (Per Serving)

- Calories: 206
- Fats: 7g
- Carbs: 28g
- Protein:12g

Kale and Chicken Soup

Serving: 4

Prep Time: 10 minutes

Cook Time: 4 minutes

Ingredients

- 2 tablespoons of clarified butter/ghee
- 1 medium-sized chopped up onion
- 3 peeled carrots cut up into bite-sized portions
- 4 stalks of celery cut up into bite-sized portions
- 2 bay leaves
- 1 teaspoon of salt
- ½ a teaspoon of black pepper
- ½ a teaspoon of dried thyme
- ¼ teaspoon of dried oregano
- 4 cups of chicken broth
- 1 pound of shredded chicken breast
- 1 large-sized handful of chopped up kale
- ½ a teaspoon of fish sauce

How To

1. Set your pot to Sauté mode and add clarified butter, allow it to heat up
2. Add onion and sauté for 5 minutes
3. Add carrots, celery, bay leaves, thyme, salt oregano, and pepper
4. sauté for 1 minute
5. Add chicken broth and enough water to reach the 6-cup margin
6. Lock up and cook on SOUP mode for 4 minutes
7. Release the pressure naturally
8. Allow the soup to rest for a minute and stir in fish sauce
9. Season with pepper and sauce and enjoy!

Nutrition Values (Per Serving)

- Calories: 229
- Fat: 13g
- Carbohydrates: 11g
- Protein: 18g

Chicken Mustard Potatoes

Serving: 4

Prep Time: 5 minutes

Cooking Time: 15 minutes

Ingredients:

- 2 pounds chicken thighs, boneless and skinless
- 3 tablespoons Dijon mustard
- 2-pound red potatoes, quartered
- 2 tablespoons olive oil
- 1 cup chicken stock
- 4 tablespoons lemon juice
- 2 tablespoons Italian seasoning
- Salt and pepper to taste

Directions:

1. Add olive oil to your Instant Pot
2. Rub salt and pepper all over chicken thighs and transfer to Instant Pot
3. Take a small bowl and add lemon juice, chicken stock, and Dijon mustard, mix well
4. Pour the mix over chicken
5. Add potatoes and Italian seasoning to the pot
6. Lock lid and cook on HIGH pressure for 15 minutes
7. Quick-release pressure
8. Serve hot and enjoy!

Nutritional Contents:

- Calories: 677
- Fat: 26g
- Carbohydrates: 37g
- Protein: 27g

Zesty Sesame Chicken

Serving: 4

Prep Time: 10 minutes

Cook Time: 25 minutes

Ingredients

- 4 chicken breasts, skinless and boneless
- Pinch of black pepper
- ½ cup yellow onions, chopped
- ½ cup coconut amino
- ¼ cup no-salt tomato sauce
- 2 tablespoons avocado oil
- 2 garlic cloves, minced
- ¼ teaspoon red pepper flakes
- 2 teaspoons sesame oil
- ½ cup honey
- 3 tablespoons water

How To

1. Add chicken, pepper, onion, tomato sauce, amino, garlic, oil, pepper flakes, sesame oil, honey, water to your pot and toss well
2. Lock lid and cook on HIGH pressure for 20 minutes
3. Release pressure naturally over 10 minutes
4. Transfer chicken to cutting board and shred using 2 forks
5. Return to pot and set your pot to Sauté mode
6. Cook for 5 minutes more
7. Serve and enjoy!

Nutrition (Per Serving)

- Calories: 251
- Fat: 4g
- Carbohydrates: 15g
- Protein: 7g

Lemon and Olive Chicken

Serving: 4

Prep Time: 5 minutes

Cook Time: 10 minutes

Ingredients

- 4 chicken breast, bones, and skin removed
- ½ teaspoon cumin
- ½ teaspoon black pepper
- 1 teaspoon salt
- ½ cup butter, melted
- Juice of 1 lemon
- 1 cup chicken broth
- 1 can pit green olives

How To

1. Take a bowl and add chicken
2. Season with cumin, pepper, and salt
3. Set your pot to Sauté mode and add chicken breast and butter
4. Brown all side for 3 minutes
5. Add remaining ingredients and lock lid
6. Cook on POULTRY mode for 10 minutes
7. Quick-release the pressure
8. Serve and enjoy!

Nutrition (Per Serving)

- Calories: 401
- Fat: 27g
- Carbohydrates: 0.8g
- Protein: 36g

Chicken with Lime Juice

Serving: 6

Prep Time: 10 minutes

Cook Time: 30 minutes

Ingredients

- 2 pounds chicken thighs, boneless
- 3 pounds red potatoes, quartered
- 2 tablespoons olive oil
- 2 tablespoons Italian seasoning
- ¼ cup lemon juice
- ¾ cup chicken broth
- 3 tablespoons Dijon mustard
- Salt and pepper

Directions

1. Add the oil and the chicken in the instant pot.
2. Sprinkle salt and pepper to taste.
3. Take a separate bowl and mix the chicken broth, lemon juice, and Dijon mustard together and mix them well.
4. Then add the potatoes cut into 4 pieces, along with the remaining seasoning.
5. Seal the instant pot lid and turn on the Manual function.
6. Cook for 15 minutes at high pressure.
7. Once cooked, allow natural release the steam for 15 minutes.
8. Serve immediately and enjoy!

Nutrition Values (Per Serving)

- Calories: 276
- Fat: 22g
- Carbohydrates: 2g
- Protein: 18g

Garlic and Herbed Turkey

Serving: 4

Prep Time: 10 minutes

Cook Time: 27 minutes

Ingredients

- 4 turkey thighs with skin and bones
- 2 teaspoons fresh thyme, chopped
- ½ cup chicken broth
- 2 teaspoons fresh oregano, chopped
- 2 tablespoons olive oil
- 8 cloves garlic, minced
- ½ cup sherry
- Salt and black pepper, to taste

Directions

1. Turn on your instant pot and set it on Sauté mode.
2. Add salt and pepper seasoning to the turkey.
3. Add olive oil in the instant pot.
4. Place the turkey thighs in the pot.
5. Cook for 5 minutes on both sides.
6. Remove the turkey thighs once it turned into golden brown.
7. Put the thyme, oregano, oil, and garlic into the pot and sauté for 2 minutes.
8. Add the sherry, chicken broth and fried turkey thighs to the pot.
9. Seal the instant pot lid.
10. Select Manual function and cook for 20 minutes at high pressure.
11. Once cooked, allow quick-release pressure to vent the steam.
12. Serve with fresh herb and enjoy!

Nutrition Values (Per Serving)

- Calories: 254
- Fat: 7g
- Carbohydrates: 12g
- Protein: 26g

Cashew Chicken

Serving: 6

Prep Time: 3 minutes

Cook Time: 15 minutes

Ingredients

- 2 pounds chicken thigh, bones and skin removed
- ¼ teaspoon black pepper
- ¼ cup of soy sauce
- 4 tablespoons rice vinegar
- 4 tablespoons of ketchup
- 1 tablespoon brown sugar
- 1 clove garlic, minced
- 1 teaspoon grated ginger
- 1 tablespoon cornstarch + 2 tablespoon water
- 1/3 cup cashew nuts, toasted
- ¼ cup green onions, chopped
- 2 tablespoons sesame seeds, toasted

How To

1. Add all of the ingredients to your Instant Pot (except cornstarch slurry, cashew, green onions, sesame seeds)
2. Gently stir
3. Lock lid and cook on HIGH pressure for 15 minutes
4. Quick-release the pressure
5. Set your pot to Sauté mode and stir in the slurry
6. Simmer until the sauce thickens
7. Stir in cashew nuts, green onions, and sesame seeds
8. Serve and enjoy!

Nutrition (Per Serving)

- Calories: 444
- Fat: 32g
- Carbohydrates: 10g
- Protein: 27g

Chapter 7: Vegetarian

Red Cabbage

Serving: 4

Prep Time: 5 minutes

Cooking Time: 10 minutes

Ingredients:

- 6 cups red cabbage, chopped
- 1 tablespoon apple cider vinegar
- ½ cup Keto-Friendly applesauce
- 1 cup of water
- 3 garlic cloves, minced
- 1 small onion, chopped
- 1 tablespoon olive oil
- Salt and pepper to taste

Directions:

1. Add olive oil to Instant Pot
2. Set it to Sauté mode and let it heat up, add onion and garlic and Sauté for 2 minutes
3. Add remaining ingredients and stir
4. Lock lid and cook on HIGH pressure for 10 minutes
5. Quick-release pressure
6. Stir well and serve
7. Enjoy!

Nutritional Contents:

- Calories: 81
- Fat: 6g
- Carbohydrates: 4g
- Protein: 2g

Asparagus Salad

Serving: 4

Prep Time: 10 minutes

Cooking Time: 20 minutes

Ingredients:

- 1 lemon juice
- 2 salmon fillets
- 1 tablespoon red wine vinegar
- 1 tablespoon walnut oil
- 1 tablespoon Dijon mustard
- ¼ cup goat parmesan cheese, shredded
- ¼ cup fresh mint
- ¼ cup pine nuts, roasted
- ¼ teaspoon pepper
- 2 cups asparagus, shaved

Directions:

1. Season salmon with salt and keep it on the side
2. Place a trivet in your Instant Pot
3. Place salmon over the trivet and close lid, cook on HIGH pressure for 15 minutes
4. Quick-release pressure
5. Transfer salmon to a platter and keep it on the side
6. Add asparagus around the salmon
7. Take a small bowl and mix lemon juice. Walnut oil, champagne vinegar, mustard and whisk well
8. Drizzle the dressing over salmon and asparagus
9. Garnish with pine nuts, pepper, mint and cheddar cheese
10. Serve and enjoy!

Nutritional Contents:

- Calories: 323
- Fat: 21g
- Carbohydrates: 4g
- Protein: 28g

Rice Cauliflower

Serving: 4

Prep Time: 5 minutes

Cooking Time: 15 minutes

Ingredients:

- 1 large cauliflower head
- 2 tablespoons olive oil
- ¼ teaspoon salt
- ½ teaspoon dried parsley
- ½ teaspoon cumin
- ¼ teaspoon turmeric
- ¼ teaspoon paprika
- Fresh cilantro
- Lime wedges

Directions:

1. Wash the cauliflower well and trim the leaves
2. Place a steamer rack on top of the pot and transfer the florets to the rack
3. Add 1 cup of water into the pot
4. Lock up the lid and cook on HIGH pressure for 1 minute
5. Once done, do a quick release
6. Transfer the flower to a serving platter
7. Set your pot to Sauté mode and add oil, allow the oil to heat up
8. Add flowers back to the pot and cook, making sure to break them using a potato masher
9. Add spices and season with a bit of salt
10. Give a nice stir and squeeze a bit of lime
11. Serve and enjoy!

Nutritional Contents:

- Calories: 169
- Fat: 14g
- Carbohydrates: 8g
- Protein: 3g

Spicy Brussels

Serving: 4

Prep Time: 5 minutes

Cooking Time: 5 minutes

Ingredients:

- 2 pounds Brussels sprouts, halved
- ¼ cup coconut amino
- 2 tablespoons sriracha sauce
- 1 tablespoon vinegar
- 2 tablespoons sesame oil
- 1 tablespoon almonds, chopped
- 1 teaspoon red pepper flakes
- 2 teaspoons garlic powder
- 1 teaspoon onion powder
- 1 tablespoon smoked paprika
- ½ tablespoons cayenne pepper
- Salt and pepper to taste

Directions:

1. Set your pot to Sauté mode and add almonds
2. Toast them for a while
3. Take a bowl and add the remaining ingredients (except the Brussels) and give it a nice mix
4. Add the Brussels to the pot alongside the prepped mixture
5. Stir well and lock up the lid
6. Cook on HIGH pressure for 3 minutes
7. Release the pressure naturally and serve!

Nutritional Contents:

- Calories: 84
- Fat: 7g
- Carbohydrates: 5g
- Protein: 2g

Pesto Zucchini

Serving: 4

Prep Time: 5 minutes

Cooking Time: 10 minutes

Ingredients:

- 1 tablespoon olive oil
- 1 onion, chopped
- 2 and ½ pound roughly chopped zucchini
- ½ cup of water
- 1 and ½ teaspoon salt
- 1 bunch basil leaves
- 2 garlic cloves, minced
- 1 tablespoon extra-virgin olive oil
- Zucchini for making zoodles

Directions:

1. Set the pot to Sauté mode and add olive oil
2. Once the oil is hot, add onion and Sauté for 4 minutes
3. Add zucchini, water, and salt
4. Lock up the lid and cook on HIGH pressure for 3 minutes
5. Release the pressure naturally
6. Add basil, garlic, and leaves
7. Use an immersion blender to blend everything well until you have a sauce-like consistency
8. Take the extra zucchini and pass them through a Spiralizer to get noodle-like shapes
9. Toss the Zoodles with sauce and enjoy!

Nutritional Contents:

- Calories: 71
- Fat: 4g
- Carbohydrates: 6g
- Protein: 3g

Coconut and Kale

Serving: 4

Prep Time: 5 minutes

Cooking Time: 5 minutes

Ingredients:

- ¼ cups of curry powder
- 1 can unsweetened coconut cream
- 1 pack dry onion soup mix
- 2 cups kale, rinsed and shredded
- 1 large yellow bell pepper, cut into strips, seeded and peeled
- 1 cup cilantro for garnish

Directions:

1. Add all the ingredients to your Instant Pot
2. Stir and lock the lid
3. Cook on HIGH pressure for 4 minutes, quick release the pressure
4. Open the lid and garnish with cilantro
5. Serve and enjoy!

Nutritional Contents:

- Calories: 433
- Fat: 42g
- Carbohydrates: 8g
- Protein: 10g

Caper and Beet Salad

Serving: 4

Prep Time: 5 minutes

Cooking Time: 25 minutes

Ingredients:

- 4 medium beets
- 2 tablespoons of rice wine vinegar

For Dressing

- Small bunch parsley, stems removed
- 1 large garlic clove
- ½ teaspoon salt
- Pinch of black pepper
- 1 tablespoon extra-virgin olive oil
- 2 tablespoons capers

Directions:

1. Pour 1 cup of water into your steamer basket and place it on the side
2. Snip up the tops of your bits and wash them well
3. Put the beets in your steamer basket
4. Place the steamer basket in your instant pot and lock up the lid
5. Let it cook for about 25 minutes at high pressure
6. Once done, release the pressure naturally
7. While it is being cooked, take a small jar and add chopped up parsley and garlic alongside olive oil, salt, pepper and capers
8. Shake it vigorously to prepared your dressing
9. Open up the lid once the pressure is released and check the beets for doneness using a fork
10. Take out the steamer basket to your sink and run it under cold water
11. Use your finger to brush off the skin of the beets
12. Use a plastic cutting board and slice up the beets
13. Arrange them on a platter and sprinkle some vinegar on top

Nutritional Contents:

- Calories: 160
- Fat: 4g
- Carbohydrates: 3g
- Protein: 2g

Chapter 8: Soups and Stews

Celery Soup

Serving: 3

Prep Time: 10 minutes

Cook Time: 30 minutes

Ingredients

- 1 large-sized celery root chopped up into 4-5 cups
- 1 medium onion, chopped
- 4 peeled garlic cloves
- 3 cups of vegetable broth (divided)
- 1/8 teaspoon of white pepper
- ½ a teaspoon of thyme
- ½ a teaspoon of salt
- ¼ cup of almond milk
- ½ a teaspoon of lemon juice

Directions

1. Peel the celery root and cut them up into equal-sized cubes
2. Set the pot to Sauté mode and add onion and garlic
3. Brown them
4. Add celery roots and 3 cups of broth
5. Lock up the lid and cook on HIGH pressure for 4 minutes
6. Allow the pressure to release naturally
7. Pour cooked celery and broth into the blender
8. Blend the mixture well until you have a smooth consistency, start from low and go to high
9. Transfer it to back to the pot
10. Add white pepper, thyme, and salt
11. Set the pot to Sauté mode and simmer for 20 minutes
12. Add almond milk and lemon juice
13. Keep stirring for 5 minutes
14. Add a bit of pepper and salt
15. Enjoy!

Nutrition Values (Per Serving)

- Calories: 214
- Fat: 13g
- Carbohydrates: 20g
- Protein: 6g

Sweet Butternut Squash Soup

Serves 8

Prep Time: 5 minutes

Cook Time: 30 minutes

Ingredients

For Soup

- 1 teaspoon of extra virgin olive oil
- 1 large onion, chopped
- 2 garlic cloves, minced
- 1 tablespoon of curry powder
- 3 pound of butternut squash, cut up into 1-inch cubes and peeled
- 3 cups of water
- ½ a cup of coconut milk

For Extra Toppings

- Hulled up pumpkin seeds
- Dried up cranberries

Directions

1. Set your pot to Sauté mode and add olive oil, allow the oil to heat up
2. Add onions and sauté for 8 minutes
3. Add garlic, curry powder and Sauté for 1 minute
4. Cancel Sauté mode and add butternut squash, water, and salt
5. Lock up the lid and cook on HIGH pressure for 30 minutes
6. Naturally, release the pressure once done
7. Open the lid and puree using an immersion blender
8. Stir in coconut milk and season with a bit of salt
9. Serve with a topping of dried cranberries and pumpkin seeds, and enjoy!

Nutrition Values (Per Serving)

- Calories: 124
- Fat: 6g
- Carbohydrates: 18g
- Protein: 2g

Kabocha Squash Soup

Serving: 6

Prep Time: 10 minutes

Cook Time: 10 minutes

Ingredients

- 8 cups of cooked Kabocha squash
- 4 cups of water
- ¼ cups of oats
- 4-6 cloves of garlic
- 1 tablespoon of seasoning
- 2 teaspoons of smoked paprika
- 1 teaspoon of curry powder
- ¼ teaspoon of ground ginger
- ¼ teaspoon of ground turmeric
- 4 cups of almond milk

How To

1. Cook the squash well
2. Cut the squash in half and deseed them
3. Add the seeded squash alongside all the other ingredients (except milk) to the pot
4. Lock up the lid and cook on HIGH pressure for 5 minutes
5. Release the pressure naturally and add almond milk
6. Puree the soup in the pot using an immersion blender
7. Set the pot to Sauté mode and Sauté for a while to thicken the soup
8. Enjoy!

Nutrition Values (Per Serving)

- Calories: 247
- Fat: 12g
- Carbohydrates: 33g
- Protein: 6g

Ultimate Leek and Corn Soup

Serving: 4

Prep Time: 10 minutes

Cooking Time: 15 minutes

Ingredients:

- 2 leeks, chopped
- 2 tablespoons butter
- 2 garlic cloves, minced
- 6 ears corn, kernels cut off, cobs reserved
- 2 bay leaves
- 4 tarragon sprigs, chopped
- 1-quart chicken stock
- Salt and pepper to taste
- A drizzle of extra virgin olive oil
- 1 tablespoon chives, chopped

Directions:

1. Set your pot to Sauté mode and add butter, let it melt
2. Add garlic and leeks, cook for 4 minutes
3. Add corn, corn cobs, bay leaves, tarragon, and stock
4. Cover everything and lock lid
5. Cook on HIGH pressure for 15 minutes
6. Release pressure naturally over 10 minutes
7. Open the lid and discard bay leaves, corn cobs and transfer the remaining to a blender
8. Pulse until you have a smooth soup
9. Season with salt and pepper
10. Stir and enjoy with a garnish of chives and olive

Nutritional Contents:

- Calories: 300
- Fat: 9g
- Carbohydrates: 50g
- Protein: 13

Barley and Mushroom Soups

Serving: 4

Prep Time: 10 minutes

Cook Time: 20 minutes

Ingredients

- 8 cups of vegetable stock
- ¾ cups of pearl barley
- 1 pound of baby Bella mushrooms, sliced up
- 1 medium onion, sliced
- 2 celery stalks, diced
- 2 diced carrots
- 4 garlic cloves, chopped
- 4 sprigs of thyme
- 1 sprig of sage
- 1 teaspoon of salt
- ¼ teaspoon of fresh ground pepper
- ¼ teaspoon of garlic powder

How To

1. Add listed ingredients to your pot
2. Stir well
3. Lock up the lid and cook on HIGH pressure for 20 minutes
4. Release the pressure naturally over 10 minutes
5. Remove the lid and give it a nice stir
6. Serve!

Nutrition Values (Per Serving)

- Calories: 263
- Fat: 12g
- Carbohydrates: 36g
- Protein: 5g

Butternut Stew

Prep Time: 10 minutes

Cooking Time: 15 minutes

Serving: 6

Ingredients

- 3 cups of vegetable broth
- 2 cups of butternut squash
- 2 cups of kidney beans, cooked
- 1 cup yellow onion, chopped
- 1 cup of yellow corn kernels
- 2 garlic cloves, minced
- 1 can of diced tomatoes
- 1 teaspoon of paprika
- 1 teaspoon of ground cumin
- 1/8 teaspoon of Ancho chili powder

How To

1. Add all of the listed ingredients to the pot
2. Lock up the lid and cook on HIGH pressure for 15 minutes
3. Release the pressure naturally
4. Remove the lid and allow it to cool
5. Enjoy!

Nutrition Values (Per Serving)

- Calories: 127
- Fat: 5g
- Carbohydrates: 20g
- Protein: 3g

White Bean Stew

Serving: 6

Prep Time: 10 minutes

Cook Time: 35 minutes

Ingredients

- 2 cups of tomatillos, chopped
- 1 cup of poblano, chopped
- 1 cup of yellow onion, chopped
- ½ of a whole jalapeno, chopped
- 1 and a ½ teaspoon of cumin, ground
- 1 and a ½ cups of great northern beans, soaked for about 12 hours, drained
- 2 teaspoons of oregano, dried
- Just a pinch of black pepper
- 1 and ½ cups of water

How To

1. Add tomatillos, onion, poblano, cumin to a blender and pulse the mixture
2. Add the mix to your Instant Pot
3. Add beans, pepper, water and toss
4. Lock up the lid and cook on HIGH pressure for 35 minutes
5. Release the pressure naturally over 10 minutes
6. Divide the mix amongst serving bowls and enjoy!

Nutrition Values (Per Serving)

- Calories: 299
- Fat: 4g
- Carbohydrates: 18g
- Protein: 6g

Cabbage and Beef Stew

Serving: 6

Prep Time: 10 minutes

Cook Time: 1 hour 20 minutes

Ingredients

- 2 and a ½ pounds of beef brisket, fat removed
- 2 bay leaves
- 4 cups of water
- 4 cups of water
- 4 carrots, chopped
- 3 garlic cloves, chopped
- 1 cabbage head, roughly shredded
- Black pepper as needed

How To

1. Add beef brisket to your Instant Pot alongside water, garlic, pepper and bay leaves
2. Lock up the lid and cook on HIGH pressure for 1 hour
3. Release the pressure naturally over 10 minutes
4. Remove the lid and add carrots, cabbage, and stir
5. Lock up the lid and cook on HIGH pressure for 6 minutes
6. Perform a quick release
7. Open the lid and divide into serving bowls
8. Enjoy!

Nutrition Values (Per Serving)

- Calories: 281
- Fat: 8g
- Carbohydrates: 21g
- Protein: 8g

Beef Broccoli Stew

Serving: 3

Prep Time: 10 minutes

Cook Time: 45 minutes

Ingredients

- ½ pound broccoli florets
- ½ cup of coconut milk
- ½ tablespoon garlic powder
- 1 tablespoon curry powder
- 1 cup chicken broth
- 1 and ¼ pounds beef stew chunks
- 1 zucchini, chopped
- ½ teaspoon salt

Directions

1. Add all the ingredients except the coconut milk into the instant pot.
2. Seal the instant pot lid and turn on the Manual function.
3. Cook for 45 minutes at high pressure.
4. Allow natural release the steam and open the lid.
5. Stir in the coconut milk.
6. Let it simmer for 2 minutes.
7. Serve immediately and enjoy!

Nutrition Values (Per Serving)

- Calories: 153
- Fat: 12g
- Carbohydrates: 6g
- Protein: 15g

Chapter 9: Fish and Seafood

Salmon and Peas

Serving: 4

Prep Time: 15 minutes

Cook Time: 15 minutes

Ingredients

- 16 ounce of salmon fillets, boneless and skin-on
- 1 tablespoon of parsley, chopped
- 10 ounces of peas
- 9 ounce of vegetable stock, low sodium
- 2 cups of water
- ½ a teaspoon of oregano, dried
- ½ a teaspoon of sweet paprika
- 2 garlic cloves, minced
- A pinch of black pepper

How To

1. Add garlic, parsley, paprika, oregano, and vegetable stock to a food processor and blend
2. Add water to your Instant Pot
3. Add steam basket
4. Add fish fillets inside the steamer basket
5. Season with pepper
6. Lock up the lid and cook on HIGH pressure for 10 minutes
7. Release the pressure naturally over 10 minutes
8. Divide the fish amongst plates
9. Add peas to the steamer basket and lock up the lid again, cook on HIGH pressure for 5 minutes
10. Quick-release the pressure
11. Divide the peas next to your fillets and serve with the parsley dressing drizzled on top
12. Enjoy!

Nutrition Values (Per Serving)

- Calories: 270
- Fat: 9g
- Carbohydrates: 32g
- Protein: 14g

Spiced Up Chili Salmon

Serving: 4

Prep Time: 10 minutes

Cook Time: 7 minutes

Ingredients

- 4 salmon fillets, boneless and skin-on
- 2 tablespoon of assorted chili peppers, chopped
- Juice of 1 lemon
- 1 lemon, sliced
- 1 cup of water
- Black pepper

How To

1. Add water to the Instant Pot
2. Add steamer basket and add salmon fillets, season the fillets with salt and pepper
3. Drizzle lemon juice on top
4. Top with lemon slices
5. Lock up the lid and cook on HIGH pressure for 7 minutes
6. Release the pressure naturally over 10 minutes
7. Divide the salmon and lemon slices between serving plates
8. Enjoy!

Nutrition Values (Per Serving)

- Calories: 281
- Fats: 8g
- Carbs: 19g
- Protein:7g

Great Prawn Chili

Servings: 4

Prep Time: 10 minutes

Cook Time: 11 minutes

Ingredients

- 1-pound prawns, shells and heads removed
- 3 onions, chopped
- 8 green chilies, chopped
- 2 tablespoons peppercorns
- 1 ½ tablespoons ginger-garlic paste
- 1 ½ tablespoons oil
- 1 ½ tablespoon cumin seeds
- 1 ½ teaspoon curry powder
- 1 teaspoon salt
- ½ cup cilantro leaves for garnish
- 1 cup of water

How To

1. Set your pot to "Sauté" mode and add oil, ginger-garlic paste, cumin seeds, peppercorns, and curry powder.
2. Sauté for 1 minute.
3. Add onions and green chilies and sauté for 4 minutes.
4. Add prawns, water, and salt.
5. Lock lid and cook on HIGH pressure for 5 minutes.
6. Release pressure naturally over 10 minutes.
7. Serve with a garnish of cilantro leaves.
8. Enjoy!

Nutritional Values (Per Serving)

- Calories: 373
- Fat: 18g
- Carbohydrates: 23g
- Protein: 30g

Shrimp and Lemon Bowl

Serving: 4

Prep Time: 10 minutes

Cook Time: 3 minutes

Ingredients

- 2 tablespoon of olive oil
- 1-pound shrimp, peeled and deveined
- 2 tablespoon of lemon juice
- Black pepper as needed
- 2 tablespoons of garlic, minced
- 1 tablespoon of lemon zest, grated
- 1 cup of water

How To

1. Set your pot to Sauté mode and add oil, allow the oil to heat up
2. Add garlic, shrimp, water, lemon juice, pepper, lemon zest, and stir
3. Lock up the lid and cook on HIGH pressure for 10 minutes
4. Release the pressure naturally over 10 minutes
5. Open the lid and divide the dish amongst the plate
6. Enjoy!

Nutrition Values (Per Serving)

- Calories: 209
- Fat: 1g
- Carbohydrates: 16g
- Protein: 9g

Steamed Salmon Fillets

Serves 2

Prep Time: 10 minutes

Cook Time: 10 minutes

Ingredients

- 2 salmon fillets
- ¼ cup onion, chopped
- 2 stalks green onion stalks, chopped
- 1 whole egg
- Almond meal as needed
- Salt and pepper to taste
- 2 tablespoons olive oil

Directions

1. Add a cup of water to your pot and place a steamer rack on top
2. Place the fish
3. Season the fish with salt and pepper and lock up the lid
4. Cook on HIGH pressure for 3 minutes
5. Once done, quick release the pressure
6. Remove the fish and allow it to cool
7. Break the fillets into a bowl and add egg, yellow and green onions
8. Add ½ a cup of almond meal and mix with your hand
9. Divide the mixture into patties
10. Take a large skillet and place it over medium heat
11. Add oil and cook the patties
12. Enjoy!

Nutrition Values (Per Serving)

- Calories: 238
- Fat: 15g
- Carbohydrates: 1g
- Protein: 23g

Broccoli and Salmon Dish

Serving: 4

Prep Time: 1 minute

Cook Time: 4 minutes

Ingredients

- 2 and a ½ ounce of Salmon Fillet
- 2 and a ½ ounce of broccoli
- 9 ounces of new potatoes
- 1 teaspoon of butter
- Pepper as needed
- Fresh herbs such as oregano, rosemary, basil, parsley, etc.

How To

1. Chop the broccoli into florets and keep them on the side
2. Add ½ a cup of water to your Instant Pot
3. Season the potatoes with salt, fresh herbs, and pepper
4. Season the salmon and broccoli with salt and pepper
5. Add potatoes to a steaming rack and smother them with butter
6. Transfer to your Instant Pot
7. Lock up the lid and cook for 2 minutes on the Steam setting
8. Quick-release the pressure
9. Add broccoli florets and salmon and steam cook for 2 minutes more
10. Quick-release
11. Serve and enjoy!

Nutrition Values (Per Serving)

- Calories: 556
- Fat: 40g
- Carbohydrates: 11g
- Protein: 39g

Mediterranean Tuna Zoodles

Serves: 2

Prep Time: 5 minutes

Cook Time: 10 minutes

Ingredients

- 1 tablespoon oil
- 1/ cup red onion, chopped
- 8 ounces zucchini zoodles
- 1 can (14.5 ounces) tomatoes diced,
- 1 teaspoon of each basil, garlic, oregano
- ¼ teaspoon salt
- 1/8 teaspoon pepper
- 1 can tuna fish
- 1 large marinated artichoke heart
- Fresh parsley, chopped
- ½ cup of water

Direction

1. Set the pot to Sauté mode and add red onions
2. Cook them for 2 minutes
3. Add Zoodles, salt, tomatoes and pour the water
4. Lock up the lid and cook on HIGH pressure for 10 minutes
5. Release the pressure naturally over 10 minutes
6. Open up the lid and add artichokes, tuna with liquid) and set your pot to Sauté mode
7. Keep stirring for 5 minutes
8. Serve and enjoy!

Nutritional Values Per Serving

- Calories: 125
- Fat: 8g
- Carbohydrates: 15g
- Protein: 6g

Kale and Salmon Salad

Serving: 4

Prep Time: 10 minutes

Cooking Time: 5 minutes

Ingredients:

- 1 lemon, juiced
- 2 salmon fillets
- ¼ cup extra virgin olive oil
- 1 teaspoon Dijon mustard
- 4 cups kale, thinly sliced, ribs removed
- 1 teaspoon salt
- 1 avocado, diced
- 1 cup pomegranate seeds
- 1 cup walnuts, toasted
- 1 cup goat parmesan cheese, shredded
- 1 teaspoon red wine vinegar

Directions:

1. Season salmon with salt and keep it on the side
2. Place a trivet in your Instant Pot
3. Place salmon over the trivet, add 1 cup water
4. Lock lid and cook on HIGH pressure for 15 minutes
5. Release pressure naturally over 10 minutes
6. Transfer salmon to a serving platter
7. Take a bowl and add kale, season with salt
8. Take another bowl and make the dressing by adding lemon juice, Dijon mustard, olive oil, and red wine vinegar
9. Season kale with dressing and add diced avocado, pomegranate seeds, walnuts and cheese
10. Toss and serve with the fish
11. Enjoy!

Nutritional Contents:

- Calories: 234
- Fat: 14g
- Carbohydrates: 12g
- Protein: 16g

Lemon Halibut

Serving: 4

Prep Time: 5 minutes

Cook Time: 8 minutes

Ingredients

- 4 halibut fillets
- 2 lemon, sliced
- 2 tablespoon chili pepper flakes
- Salt and pepper as needed

How To

1. Place a trivet in the Instant Pot
2. Add a cup of water
3. Season halibut fillets with chili pepper flakes, pepper, and salt
4. Place halibut on a trivet and arrange slices of lemon on top of the halibut
5. Close lid and cook on HIGH pressure for 8 minutes
6. Release the pressure over 10 minutes
7. Enjoy!

Nutrition (Per Serving)

- Calories: 395
- Fat: 23g
- Carbohydrates: 4g
- Protein: 42g

Juicy Poached Salmon

Serving: 4

Prep Time: 3 minutes

Cook Time: 4 minutes

Ingredients

- 4 pieces of 16-ounce salmon fillet, skin on
- 4 scallions, chopped
- Zest of 1 lemon
- ½ a teaspoon of fennel seeds
- 1 teaspoon white wine vinegar
- 1 bay leaf
- ½ cup dry white wine
- 2 cups chicken broth
- ¼ cup fresh dill
- Salt and pepper

How To

1. Add the listed ingredients to your Instant Pot
2. Stir gently
3. Lock lid and cook on HIGH pressure for 4 minutes
4. Release the pressure naturally over 10 minutes
5. Serve and enjoy!

Nutrition (Per Serving)

- Calories: 631
- Fat: 24g
- Carbohydrates: 4g
- Protein: 0.7g

Chapter 10: Desserts

Carrot Halwa

Servings: 3

Prep Time: 10 minutes

Cook Time: 15 minutes

Ingredients

- 12 carrots, peeled and grated
- 2 tablespoons ghee
- 1 cup milk
- ½ cup of sugar
- 4 cardamoms
- 2 tablespoons almonds, sliced
- 2 tablespoons raisins

How To

1. Add grated carrots and ghee.
2. Set your pot to "Sauté" mode and cook for 2-3 minutes.
3. Add milk and lock lid.
4. Cook on HIGH pressure for 5 minutes.
5. Perform quick release.
6. Add sugar and cardamom.
7. Sauté for 7 minutes more until the liquid has almost evaporated.
8. Garnish with sliced almonds and raisins.
9. Enjoy!

Nutritional Values (Per Serving)

- Calories: 385
- Fat: 12g
- Carbohydrates: 67g
- Protein: 6g

Avocado and Coconut Pudding

Serving: 4

Prep Time: 10 minutes

Cook Time: 5 minutes

Ingredients

- 2 avocados, pitted, peeled and chopped
- 2 teaspoons of vanilla extract
- 2 tablespoon of coconut sugar
- 1 tablespoon of lime juice
- 14-ounce coconut milk
- 1 and ½ cups of water

How To

1. Take a bowl and add avocado, coconut sugar, vanilla extract, coconut milk, lime juice, and blend well
2. Pour the mixture into a ramekin (small enough to fit inside your pot)
3. Add water to your Instant Pot
4. Place a steamer basket and place the pot in the basket
5. Lock up the lid and cook on HIGH pressure for 5 minutes
6. Release the pressure naturally over 10 minutes
7. Take it out and serve chilled, enjoy!

Nutrition Values (Per Serving)

- Calories: 190
- Fat: 3g
- Carbohydrates: 13g
- Protein: 4g

Delicious Coconut Pudding

Servings: 3

Prep Time: 10 minutes

Cook Time: 10 minutes

Ingredients

- 2 cups of milk
- 1 coconut, shredded and ground
- 1 cup of coconut water
- ½ cup gelatin
- 1 can condensed milk
- 1 drop vanilla essence
- 8 tablespoons sugar

How To

1. Set your pot to "Sauté" mode, adding coconut water and gelatin.
2. Sauté for 3 minutes.
3. Take a saucepan and place it over medium heat. Add condensed milk, sugar and bring to a boil.
4. Add mixture to Instant Pot and add vanilla essence.
5. Sauté for 2 minutes more.
6. Add grated coconut.
7. Serve and enjoy!

Nutritional Values (Per Serving)

- Calories: 385
- Fat: 11g
- Carbohydrates: 62g
- Protein: 11g

Cheesy Popcorns

Serving: 6

Prep Time: 5 minutes

Cooking Time: 5 minutes

Ingredients:

- 1 tablespoons garlic puree
- ½ cup corn
- 1 and ¼ cup cheddar cheese
- 2 teaspoon coconut oil
- Salt to taste

Directions:

1. Select sauté mode
2. Add coconut oil and heat up
3. Add corn, garlic and salt then stir
4. Secure the lid properly
5. Let the corns pop up 2-3 minutes
6. After finishing popping, add grated cheese and let it melt
7. Serve and enjoy!

Nutritional Contents:

- Calories: 154
- Fat: 4g
- Carbohydrates: 10g
- Protein: 10g

Simple Applesauce

Serving: 10

Prep Time: 10 minutes

Cooking Time: Nil

Ingredients:

- 12 apples. Peeled and cored
- ½ cup corn

Directions:

1. Add listed ingredients to your instant pot
2. Take a piece of parchment paper over the apples
3. Secure the lid properly
4. Cook on High for 10 minutes
5. Release the pressure naturally for 10 minutes
6. Transfer them into your food processor
7. Blend until smooth
8. Serve and enjoy!

Nutritional Contents:

- Calories: 145
- Fat: 0.5g
- Carbohydrates: 38g
- Protein: 0.7g

Peaches and Oats

Serving: 4

Prep Time: 5 minutes

Cooking Time: 8 minutes

Ingredients:

- 2 peaches, diced
- 1 cup coconut milk
- ½ vanilla bean pod, scraped
- 1 cup steel cut oats
- 2 cups water

Directions:

1. Put everything in inner pot
2. Lock the lid properly
3. Set to High pressure for 3 minutes
4. Once cooked, let the pressure vent using NPR method for 10 minutes
5. Then open the steam valve and release the remaining pressure
6. Serve and enjoy!

Nutritional Contents:

- Calories: 154
- Fat: 2g
- Carbohydrates: 5g
- Protein: 3g

Creamy Peach with Oats

Serving: 4

Prep Time: 5 minutes

Cooking Time: 5 minutes

Ingredients:

- 1 peach, chopped
- 2 cups oats, rolled
- 1 teaspoon vanilla
- 4 cups water

Toppings:

- Splash milk, cream or non-dairy milk
- ½ cup almonds, chopped
- Maple syrup, to taste
- 2 tablespoons flax meal

Directions:

1. Put everything in inner pot
2. Lock the lid properly
3. Set to PORRIDGE High pressure for 3 minutes
4. Once cooked, let the pressure vent using NPR method for 10 minutes
5. Then open the steam valve and release the remaining pressure
6. Serve and enjoy!

Nutritional Contents:

- Calories: 154
- Fat: 2g
- Carbohydrates: 5g
- Protein: 3g

Baked Potatoes

Serving: 8

Prep Time: 2-3 minutes

Cooking Time: 30 minutes

Ingredients:

- 1 cup water
- 5 pounds potatoes

Directions:

1. Set your IP trivet in the inner pot then pour the water
2. Put potatoes on the rack
3. Lock the lid properly
4. Set to Manual for 10 minutes
5. Once cooked, let the pressure vent using NPR method for 20 minutes
6. Then open the steam valve and release the remaining pressure
7. Serve and enjoy!

Nutritional Contents:

- Calories: 154
- Fat: 2g
- Carbohydrates: 5g
- Protein: 3g

Ham and Spinach

Serving: 4

Prep Time: 5 minutes

Cooking Time: 20 minutes

Ingredients:

- 1 onion, chopped
- 1-pound ham uncured, fully cooked, chunked to large pieces
- 2 cloves garlic, crushed
- 1 tablespoon olive oil
- 6 cups spinach
- 1 turnip, chopped
- ½ cup low sodium chicken broth
- 1/8 teaspoon salt

Directions:

1. Put everything in inner pot
2. Lock the lid properly
3. Set to Manual High pressure for 20 minutes
4. Once cooked, let the pressure vent using NPR method for 10 minutes
5. Then open the steam valve and release the remaining pressure
6. Stir the ingredients to mix well
7. Serve and enjoy!

Nutritional Contents:

- Calories: 154
- Fat: 2g
- Carbohydrates: 5g
- Protein: 3g

Baked Apples

Serving: 6

Prep Time: 5 minutes

Cooking Time: 10 minutes

Ingredients:

- 6 apples, cored
- 1 cup red wine
- ¼ cup raisins
- ½ cup sugar
- 1 teaspoon cinnamon, powdered

Directions:

1. Put everything in inner pot
2. Lock the lid properly
3. Set to Manual High pressure for 10 minutes
4. Once cooked, let the pressure vent using NPR method for 10 to 15 minutes
5. Then open the steam valve and release the remaining pressure
6. Take a serving bowl and scoop the apples then pour with lots of the cooking liquid
7. Serve and enjoy!

Nutritional Contents:

- Calories: 154
- Fat: 2g
- Carbohydrates: 5g
- Protein: 3g

Simple Coconut Cake

Serving: 6

Prep Time: 5 minutes

Cooking Time: 10 minutes

Ingredients:

Dry Ingredients

- 1 cup almond flour
- ½ cup unsweetened shredded coconut
- 1/3 cup Truvia
- 1 teaspoon of apple pie spice
- 1 teaspoon of baking powder

Wet Ingredients

- ¼ cup melted butter
- 2 lightly whisked eggs
- ½ cup heavy whipping cream

Directions:

1. Add all dry ingredients in a bowl and add the wet ingredients one at a time, making sure to gently stir after each addition
2. Empty batter into a pan and cover with foil
3. Add water 1-2 cups of water to Instant Pot, place steamer rack
4. Place pan in a steamer rack and lock lid
5. Cook on HIGH pressure for 40 minutes
6. Naturally, release the pressure over 10 minutes
7. Quick-release pressure
8. Remove pan and let it cool for 15-20 minutes
9. Flip it over onto a platter and garnish as needed
10. Serve and enjoy!

Nutritional Contents:

- Calories: 236
- Fat: 23g
- Carbohydrates: 3g
- Protein: 5g

Coconut and Figs

Serving: 2

Prep Time: 6 minutes

Cook Time: 4 minutes

Ingredients

- 2 tablespoons fat-free coconut butter
- 12 figs, halved
- ¼ cup palm sugar
- 1 cup walnuts, toasted and chopped
- 1 cup of water

How To

1. Add butter, figs, sugar, walnut, waters to your Instant Pot and toss
2. Close lid and cook on HIGH pressure for 4 minutes
3. Quick-release pressure
4. Divide mix amongst serving bowls and serve
5. Enjoy!

Nutrition (Per Serving)

- Calories: 200
- Fat: 2g
- Carbohydrates: 12g
- Protein: 9g

Conclusion

I would like to thank you again for purchasing the book and taking the time to go through the book as well.

I do hope that this book has been helpful and you found the information contained within the scriptures useful!

Keep in mind that you are not only limited to the recipes provided in this book! Just go ahead and keep on exploring until you find the best Weight Watchers Freestyle regime that works for you with your amazing Instant Pot!

Stay healthy and stay safe!

48358924R00062

Made in the USA
San Bernardino, CA
16 August 2019